ABSTINENCE

A TURN BY
LANFORD WILSON

★

★

DRAMATISTS
PLAY SERVICE
INC.

ABSTINENCE was first presented on October 24, 1988, by Circle Repertory Company as part of their Twentieth Anniversary Celebration gala benefit honoring Lanford Wilson. It was directed by Marshall W. Mason with the following cast:

MARTHA. . . . . Bobo Lewis
DANNA. . . . . Debra Mooney
WINNIE. . . . . Mary McDonnell
LON. . . . . .Mark Blum
JOE. . . . . Steve Bassett

" . . . Abstinence engenders maladies."
Love's Labour's Lost

CHARACTERS

MARTHA, THE MAID — A maid.
LON — Winnie's husband. 35 and mild.
WINNIE — Thirty, sweet and charming. Always.
DANNA — Thirty. Sharp and a little hysterical just tonight.
JOE — Thirty. The All American Sweetheart of a man. Unfortunately mad.

SCENE

The very dark front hall of a New York apartment. Maybe track lighting. Chic.

Abstinence

Martha, the Maid, stands at the front door. Lon enters, lighting a cigarette.

LON. I think all the guests are here, Martha.

MARTHA. Is this the shoplifters or the smokers or the sex-offenders or the drunks?

LON. I think it's the weight-watchers, but just in case it's the smokers I stepped out here to have a cigarette.

WINNIE. (*Enters from another way.*) Happy anniversary, darling. I'm so thankful you're here.

LON. Happy anniversary, Winnie. My helpful little helpless wife. I thought you were in with your guests.

WINNIE. I just popped up for a moment to tuck in the children.

LON. Why is it that every anniversary we have to give a party for one of your charity groups?

WINNIE. I just feel our life is so perfect we should help those less fortunate. (*They exit arm-in-arm.*)

MARTHA. (*To the audience.*) Already you know we're in trouble, right? (*The doorbell rings. Martha reaches to open it, turns to look at audience.*) One tip. Always bet on somebody named Winnie. (*She opens the door. Danna staggers in a step.*)

DANNA. Thank God someone's here! You're not Winnie. You're . . . she talks about you all the time . . . you're Abigail or Eleanor or Lady Bird. . . .

MARTHA. Martha.

DANNA. Martha!

MARTHA. And whom should I say . . . ?

DANNA. Oh. I'm a friend. I've just come from a meeting — this is the closest place I could think of. Tell her — My name is — God, I knew it a minute ago. Danna! I'm Danna Walsh.

MARTHA. Danna Walsh. (*In one move Martha takes a book from nowhere, pages quickly to the back, checks, raises her eyebrows.*)

DANNA. Now, Jackie, darling . . .

MARTHA. Martha.

DANNA. Martha, darling, you've got to get me a drink.

MARTHA. No way.

DANNA. I'll give you money. I'll give you my jewels. I'll give you my husband—no, I dumped him, I'll give you my mother.

MARTHA. I was weakening but you blew it.

WINNIE. (*Entering.*) Martha, who was at — Danna, darling! I so wanted to be there for you tonight but we have this dinner party every year.

DANNA. I hate to burst in on you like this but you've always been so helpful. I have to talk to you alone.

WINNIE. Oh, Martha knows everything.

DANNA. You do? (*Beat. Goes to Martha.*) What is a . . . (*Whispers. Martha raises her eyebrows, whispers back into Danna's ear.*) Well, of course it is. It's absurdly simple if you think about it. (*To Winnie.*) Winnie, you've got to help me.

WINNIE. You don't look well at all. How did it go?

DANNA. How did what go?

WINNIE. The meeting. A.A. The first anniversary of your sobriety.

DANNA. Who remembers, it must have been twenty minutes ago. I was a wreck. I qualified. Everyone applauded. I could have ripped their hearts out. I was congratulated. The rich bitch who runs things called be a brick. I've never wanted a drink so badly in my life.

WINNIE. Don't be silly. We're all so proud of you! You've gone an entire year today without a drink.

DANNA. A year? Are you mad? What would be so unusual about that? This is leap year you idiot. Three hundred sixty-six long tedious days. And three hundred sixty long hopeless nights. I've read over five hundred books. I've written four. I've knitted some things: a bed cover, wallpaper for the living room. Johnnie Walker Red! Now there's a man with spine. Aren't you going to ask me in?

WINNIE. You're in, darling.

DANNA. This is your apartment? This well? It's pitch in here!

WINNIE. Would you like a cup of tea?

DANNA. (*All hope gone. Musing.*) Oh . . . no . . . I've

6

been haunted all day by a scene in one of the Thin Man movies. Nick is at the table when Nora comes in late, and she asks him how much he's had to drink; Nick says he's had five martinis. And when the waiter comes over Nora says, "Would you please bring me five martinis?" (*Beat.*) I want to live like that. I want charm in my life. I want my alcohol back. I used to have a wonderful life. I mean, I didn't have friends, but I didn't notice.

WINNIE. Why don't you come join us? Just twenty or so, they're sitting down to eat. They're Liars, I'm afraid, Liars Anonymous, but you know how charming they can be.

DANNA. Food? How shallow. People I don't know? Without a drink? I'll just steady myself against the wall here— where is it?—and I'll be fine. If Dolly could just bring me a . . .

MARTHA. Forget it.

WINNIE. I know, love. I'm a drunk, too. I've had some—

DANNA. Ha! You call yourself a drunk? You haven't had a drink in three years. Put me in front of a bottle of Cuervo Gold and I'll show you a drunk.

WINNIE. You know what we say: One day at a time.

DANNA. I've experienced one day at a time for three hundred sixty-six days—end to end. Twenty-four hours in every day, eighty-six thousand four hundred seconds. I know, I counted them once. A year ago I could celebrate the Fourth of July, come home, go to bed, wake up, it would be November.

LON. (*Enters. Sees Danna, maybe hesitates one step, smiles.*) Winnie, are you coming back to the . . .

WINNIE. Lon, I want you to meet a dear friend of mine. This is Danna. We've been friends for, oh, my, how long is it?

DANNA. Three hundred sixty-six . . . endless . . .

WINNIE. Is it a year already? Danna, this is my husband, Lon.

DANNA. You don't happen to be carrying, do you?

WINNIE. Danna was just admiring the foyer.

LON. Yes, my wife did the entire apartment herself.

DANNA. I haven't seen it.

LON. I was just talking to the most remarkable man in there. He says he climbed Mount Everest completely by himself.

7

WINNIE. Let me just — oh, you know what a terrible organizer I am — I'll just get the next course started and then I'm all yours. (*She goes out, smiling. Just before she leaves she stops. Thinks. Looks at Martha, then goes out thinking. A calm beat. You can't tell, but they are listening to Winnie's retreat.*)

DANNA. (*They stare at each other an intense moment. Then:*) Alonzo! (*They kiss passionately, fall to the ground in a 69 position, Lon's head up Danna's dress, both growling and barking like dogs. They sit up. Danna's hair is a mess. They stare at each other a frozen beat.*)

MARTHA. (*To audience.*) I turned down a paying job to do this play.

LON. (*To Danna.*) Every moment without you has been hell!

DANNA. You can't possibly be Winnie's husband. You're that pompous miser she talks about? She said you were eighty! She said you had no teeth.

LON. Where did you meet Winnie?

DANNA. Ha! You think she really goes to ballet class five times a week? Have you once asked to see her plie? You told me your wife was Catholic, blind, and confined to a wheelchair.

LON. I didn't want to worry you.

DANNA. I mean she's a kind-hearted helpless thing, but you might have told me you were married to Miss Ripple of 1985.

LON. Don't be jealous, Danna. Winnie never drinks.

DANNA. Ha! I could tell you stories about that Sweet-pea that would turn your piss green. Ever wonder why she carried a sewing basket for twelve years without ever so much as darning a sock?

LON. Winnie is the most charitable woman in the city.

DANNA. If you mean she's known for giving it away.

LON. This is not becoming, Danna.

DANNA. She can't help it, poor dear. While you're down on Wall Street that poor helpless thing is down on half of Spanish Harlem.

LON. You could hardly know her.

DANNA. I know you have two olive-skinned sons with flashing black eyes.

LON. (*Moving closer, becoming aroused.*) If anything, Winnie is almost too gentle and kind. She has none of the shocking terms of endearment that you have. Or the voracious appetite. None of the inventive positions . . . certainly none of the improvisationally creative — before I met you I had no idea of the things that could be done with raw vegetables. If I were to think one of you had a broad experience . . .

DANNA. I wasn't myself, Lon. I was sober. And as for the potato trick, I learned that one at . . . (*Remembering herself.*) I mean to say . . . "Winnie" you said her name was? No, we've only met a couple of times. Meetings or something, a few friends. I had no idea she was your wife. I doubt that I could allow myself to see you again now that I know — (*Losing it.*) —unless you either take me right here in this dungeon of a foyer or bring me a Manhattan. Oh, god! With a Manhattan who needs a man? A Manhattan asks nothing from you. It doesn't deceive or sulk or play games. And it has, God knows, more interesting conversation. A Manhattan . . . listens!

LON. (*Love talk.*) You said to pick —

WINNIE. (*He shuts up as she enters, she notices but doesn't show it.*) Now, I'm all yours.

DANNA. Winnie! You poor deceived darling. You weak and caring . . .

WINNIE. Could you wait just a little moment? (*She exits.*)

LON. (*Adjusting back.*) You said to pick up a zuccini . . . I got three. And a cucumber. And a baby eggplant. And a crooked necked squash. The mind boggles.

DANNA. (*Torn, but.*) Woah . . . no, no Lon. It's not enough. The night with the pumpkin was fun, but it's not enough.

LON. Martha might ask the cook if she has any sherry.

MARTHA. This woman is loaded for bear, she'd blow a glass of sherry to hell.

LON. Really, I don't believe there's any alcohol in the house.

DANNA. You're goddamned right there isn't. You'll find there's no nail polish remover either. That tit-mouse wouldn't trust herself in the same room with vanilla extract. Why do you think the radiator kept freezing on your car? It's the trusting ones who need our help, Alonzo. She needs you. A charming intelligent dynamo of a man who inherited thirty-seven million and has parleyed that, now, into . . . how much?

LON. (*Proud.*) Well . . . a little over twelve. But I could never leave you. You're special. Who else has a living room with cable-knit walls?

DANNA. (*Pleased.*) For one, my mother. I did hers too.

LON. But, you're right. Winnie does need me.

DANNA. If it were anyone but that lovely, un-complicated . . .

LON. But she doesn't have to know.

DANNA. The woman has gimlet eyes. She's been sober for three years, she can see through six feet of concrete. (*Winnie enters with Joe, a very handsome young man indeed.*)

WINNIE. Danna, darling. I wanted you to meet Joe. Joe is a friend of Bill Wilson's too.

JOE. Sorry, Winnie, I'd love to meet the fellow but I don't know Bill Wilson at all. Sounds like a lovely guy. Do you?

DANNA. Know him? I've practically had his child. If he were here I'd saute the sanctimonious son-of-a-bitch in Mar-sala. Whoever — (*She notices Joe for the first time and does not take her eyes off him again.*) Oh. Hi, Joe.

JOE. Hi.

DANNA. You're leaving soon?

JOE. I don't know. My pilot had the jet warmed up to go to Buenos Aires, but I saw you in the hall here and called him to cancel the trip.

DANNA. And then, Buenos Aires is so . . . hot this time of year.

JOE. And I don't like to fly without a drink and my doctor says my liver's shot. All those years in the P.O.W. camps.

DANNA. You poor dear. What was your drink? Bourbon?

JOE. Well, since we have our own vineyards, I mostly just stick to Dom Perignon. Family loyalty and all that.

DANNA. With me it's a cold vodka martini. Or two.

JOE. Twist or an olive?

DANNA. Hold the garbage.

JOE. So this is your anniversary.

DANNA. My first. It's been little nervous-making.

WINNIE. Remember, you don't have to worry about to-morrow. You just have to get through tonight.

10

DANNA. Oh, suddenly, I don't think that's going to be such a problem. —I don't know though. You sound like a playboy.

JOE. Actually, I'm a physicist.

DANNA. My. (*Winnie is helping Joe on with his coat.*)

JOE. And you live close-by.

DANNA. Twenty or thirty blocks.

LON. Danna? Aren't you going to say goodnight? Danna? The crisper?

WINNIE. Oh. And Joe.

JOE. Yes, Winnie?

WINNIE. Happy anniversary.

JOE. Thanks.

DANNA. It's your anniversary too?

JOE. Well, I don't talk about it. My wife, the Dutchess, had a passion for collecting Iranian pottery. Nothing would do but she had to go there just one more time.

DANNA. Oh no.

JOE. Caught in a terrorist crossfire.

DANNA. You don't have to talk about it.

JOE. Should we walk?

DANNA. Let's take a cab. (*They leave.*)

WINNIE. (*After a beat.*) I do hope she'll be alright.

LON. You worry too much about other people. She can look after herself. Not like my helpless darling. It's his anniversary, too?

WINNIE. Yes. Such a pity. But they let him out this one night every year. We must go in and join our guests . . . take my arm. Now, remember, this is my Liars Anonymous group; don't believe a word anyone says . . . Darling. I was looking in the refrigerator. You must show me what you plan to do with all those vegetables. (*Martha is left alone as at the beginning. A pause.*)

MARTHA. . . . "The night with the pumpkin . . . was fun? . . . " (*Beat.*) Liars Anonymous. Wouldn't you know. I had two marriage proposals and a tip on the market from that group. (*Going.*) What a nasty little play. I don't know about you but I'll never touch a crudité again. (*Gone.*)

END

11

NEW PLAYS

★ **INTIMATE APPAREL by Lynn Nottage.** The moving and lyrical story of a turn-of-the-century black seamstress whose gifted hands and sewing machine are the tools she uses to fashion her dreams from the whole cloth of her life's experiences. "…Nottage's play has a delicacy and eloquence that seem absolutely right for the time she is depicting…" *–NY Daily News.* "…thoughtful, affecting…The play offers poignant commentary on an era when the cut and color of one's dress—and of course, skin—determined whom one could and could not marry, sleep with, even talk to in public." *–Variety.* [2M, 4W] ISBN: 0-8222-2009-1

★ **BROOKLYN BOY by Donald Margulies.** A witty and insightful look at what happens to a writer when his novel hits the bestseller list. "The characters are beautifully drawn, the dialogue sparkles…" *–nytheatre.com.* "Few playwrights have the mastery to smartly investigate so much through a laugh-out-loud comedy that combines the vintage subject matter of successful writer-returning-to-ethnic-roots with the familiar mid-life crisis." *–Show Business Weekly.* [4M, 3W] ISBN: 0-8222-2074-1

★ **CROWNS by Regina Taylor.** Hats become a springboard for an exploration of black history and identity in this celebratory musical play. "Taylor pulls off a Hat Trick: She scores thrice, turning CROWNS into an artful amalgamation of oral history, fashion show, and musical theater…" *–TheatreMania.com.* "…wholly theatrical…Ms. Taylor has created a show that seems to arise out of spontaneous combustion, as if a bevy of department-store customers simultaneously decided to stage a revival meeting in the changing room." *–NY Times.* [1M, 6W (2 musicians)] ISBN: 0-8222-1963-8

★ **EXITS AND ENTRANCES by Athol Fugard.** The story of a relationship between a young playwright on the threshold of his career and an aging actor who has reached the end of his. "[Fugard] can say more with a single line than most playwrights convey in an entire script…Paraphrasing the title, it's safe to say this drama, making its memorable entrance into our consciousness, is unlikely to exit as long as a theater exists for exceptional work." *–Variety.* "A thought-provoking, elegant and engrossing new play…" *–Hollywood Reporter.* [2M] ISBN: 0-8222-2041-5

★ **BUG by Tracy Letts.** A thriller featuring a pair of star-crossed lovers in an Oklahoma City motel facing a bug invasion, paranoia, conspiracy theories and twisted psychological motives. "…obscenely exciting…top-flight craftsmanship. Buckle up and brace yourself…" *–NY Times.* "…[a] thoroughly outrageous and thoroughly entertaining play…the possibility of enemies, real and imagined, to squash has never been more theatrical." *–A.P.* [3M, 2W] ISBN: 0-8222-2016-4

★ **THOM PAIN (BASED ON NOTHING) by Will Eno.** An ordinary man muses on childhood, yearning, disappointment and loss, as he draws the audience into his last-ditch plea for empathy and enlightenment. "It's one of those treasured nights in the theater—treasured nights anywhere, for that matter—that can leave you both breathless with exhilaration and…in a puddle of tears." *–NY Times.* "Eno's words…are familiar, but proffered in a way that is constantly contradictory to our expectations. Beckett is certainly among his literary ancestors." *–nytheatre.com.* [1M] ISBN: 0-8222-2076-8

★ **THE LONG CHRISTMAS RIDE HOME by Paula Vogel.** Past, present and future collide on a snowy Christmas Eve for a troubled family of five. "…[a] lovely and hauntingly original family drama…a work that breathes so much life into the theater." *–Time Out.* "…[a] delicate visual feast…" *–NY Times.* "…brutal and lovely…the overall effect is magical." *–NY Newsday.* [3M, 3W] ISBN: 0-8222-2003-2

DRAMATISTS PLAY SERVICE, INC.
440 Park Avenue South, New York, NY 10016 212-683-8960 Fax 212-213-1539
postmaster@dramatists.com www.dramatists.com

NEW PLAYS

★ **MATCH by Stephen Belber.** Mike and Lisa Davis interview a dancer and choreographer about his life, but it is soon evident that their agenda will either ruin or inspire them—and definitely change their lives forever. "Prolific laughs and ear-to-ear smiles." *–NY Magazine.* "Uproariously funny, deeply moving, enthralling theater. Stephen Belber's MATCH has great beauty and tenderness, and abounds in wit." *–NY Daily News.* "Three and a half out of four stars." *–USA Today.* "A theatrical steeplechase that leads straight from outrageous bitchery to unadorned, heartfelt emotion." *–Wall Street Journal.* [2M, 1W] ISBN: 0-8222-2020-2

★ **HANK WILLIAMS: LOST HIGHWAY by Randal Myler and Mark Harelik.** The story of the beloved and volatile country-music legend Hank Williams, featuring twenty-five of his most unforgettable songs. "[LOST HIGHWAY has] the exhilarating feeling of Williams on stage in a particular place on a particular night…serves up classic country with the edges raw and the energy hot…By the end of the play, you've traveled on a profound emotional journey: LOST HIGHWAY transports its audience and communicates the inspiring message of the beauty and richness of Williams' songs…forceful, clear-eyed, moving, impressive." *–Rolling Stone.* "…honors a very particular musical talent with care and energy… smart, sweet, poignant." *–NY Times.* [7M, 3W] ISBN: 0-8222-1985-9

★ **THE STORY by Tracey Scott Wilson.** An ambitious black newspaper reporter goes against her editor to investigate a murder and finds the *best* story…but at what cost? "A singular new voice…deeply emotional, deeply intellectual, and deeply musical…" *–The New Yorker.* "…a conscientious and absorbing new drama…" *–NY Times.* "…a riveting, tough-minded drama about race, reporting and the truth…" *–A.P.* "… a stylish, attention-holding script that ends on a chilling note that will leave viewers with much to talk about." *–Curtain Up.* [2M, 7W (doubling, flexible casting)] ISBN: 0-8222-1998-0

★ **OUR LADY OF 121st STREET by Stephen Adly Guirgis.** The body of Sister Rose, beloved Harlem nun, has been stolen, reuniting a group of life-challenged childhood friends who square off as they wait for her return. "A scorching and dark new comedy… Mr. Guirgis has one of the finest imaginations for dialogue to come along in years." *–NY Times.* "Stephen Guirgis may be the best playwright in America under forty." *–NY Magazine.* [8M, 4W] ISBN: 0-8222-1965-4

★ **HOLLYWOOD ARMS by Carrie Hamilton and Carol Burnett.** The coming-of-age story of a dreamer who manages to escape her bleak life and follow her romantic ambitions to stardom. Based on Carol Burnett's bestselling autobiography, *One More Time.* "…pure theatre and pure entertainment…" *–Talkin' Broadway.* "…a warm, fuzzy evening of theatre." *–BrodwayBeat.com.* "…chuckles and smiles of recognition or surprise flow naturally…a remarkable slice of life." *–TheatreScene.net.* [5M, 5W, 1 girl] ISBN: 0-8222-1959-X

★ **INVENTING VAN GOGH by Steven Dietz.** A haunting and hallucinatory drama about the making of art, the obsession to create and the fine line that separates truth from myth. "Like a van Gogh painting, Dietz's story is a gorgeous example of excess—one that remakes reality with broad, well-chosen brush strokes. At evening's end, we're left with the author's resounding opinions on art and artifice, and provoked by his constant query into which is greater: van Gogh's art or his violent myth." *–Phoenix New Times.* "Dietz's writing is never simple. It is always brilliant. Shaded, compressed, direct, lucid—he frames his subject with a remarkable understanding of painting as a physical experience." *–Tucson Citizen.* [4M, 1W] ISBN: 0-8222-1954-9

DRAMATISTS PLAY SERVICE, INC.
440 Park Avenue South, New York, NY 10016 212-683-8960 Fax 212-213-1539
postmaster@dramatists.com www.dramatists.com

NEW PLAYS

★ **THE EXONERATED by Jessica Blank and Erik Jensen.** Six interwoven stories paint a picture of an American criminal justice system gone horribly wrong and six brave souls who persevered to survive it. "The #1 play of the year...intense and deeply affecting..." –*NY Times.* "Riveting. Simple, honest storytelling that demands reflection." –*A.P.* "Artful and moving...pays tribute to the resilience of human hearts and minds." –*Variety.* "Stark...riveting...cunningly orchestrated." –*The New Yorker.* "Hard-hitting, powerful, and socially relevant." –*Hollywood Reporter.* [7M, 3W] ISBN: 0-8222-1946-8

★ **STRING FEVER by Jacquelyn Reingold.** Lily juggles the big issues: turning forty, artificial insemination and the elusive scientific Theory of Everything in this Off-Broadway comedy hit. "Applies the elusive rules of string theory to the conundrums of one woman's love life. Think *Sex and the City* meets *Copenhagen.*" –*NY Times.* "A funny offbeat and touching look at relationships...an appealing romantic comedy populated by oddball characters." –*NY Daily News.* "Where kooky, zany, and madcap meet...whimsically winsome." –*NY Magazine.* "STRING FEVER will have audience members happily stringing along." –*TheaterMania.com.* "Reingold's language is surprising, inventive, and unique." –*nytheatre.com.* "...[a] whimsical comic voice." –*Time Out.* [3M, 3W (doubling)] ISBN: 0-8222-1952-2

★ **DEBBIE DOES DALLAS adapted by Erica Schmidt, composed by Andrew Sherman, conceived by Susan L. Schwartz.** A modern morality tale told as a comic musical of tragic proportions as the classic film is brought to the stage. "A scream! A saucy, tongue-in-cheek romp." –*The New Yorker.* "Hilarious! DEBBIE manages to have it all: beauty, brains and a great sense of humor!" –*Time Out.* "Shamelessly silly, shrewdly self-aware and proud of being naughty. Great fun!" –*NY Times.* "Racy and raucous, a lighthearted, fast-paced thoroughly engaging and hilarious send-up." –*NY Daily News.* [3M, 5W] ISBN: 0-8222-1955-7

★ **THE MYSTERY PLAYS by Roberto Aguirre-Sacasa.** Two interrelated one acts, loosely based on the tradition of the medieval mystery plays. "... stylish, spine-tingling...Mr. Aguirre-Sacasa uses standard tricks of horror stories, borrowing liberally from masters like Kafka, Lovecraft, Hitchcock...But his mastery of the genre is his own...irresistible." –*NY Times.* "Undaunted by the special-effects limitations of theatre, playwright and *Marvel* comicbook writer Roberto Aguirre-Sacasa maps out some creepy twilight zones in THE MYSTERY PLAYS, an engaging, related pair of one acts...The theatre may rarely deliver shocks equivalent to, say, *Dawn of the Dead,* but Aguirre-Sacasa's work is fine compensation." –*Time Out.* [4M, 2W] ISBN: 0-8222-2038-5

★ **THE JOURNALS OF MIHAIL SEBASTIAN by David Auburn.** This epic one-man play spans eight tumultuous years and opens a uniquely personal window on the Romanian Holocaust and the Second World War. "Powerful." –*NY Times.* "[THE JOURNALS OF MIHAIL SEBASTIAN] allows us to glimpse the idiosyncratic effects of that awful history on one intelligent, pragmatic, recognizably real man..." –*NY Newsday.* [3M, 5W] ISBN: 0-8222-2006-7

★ **LIVING OUT by Lisa Loomer.** The story of the complicated relationship between a Salvadoran nanny and the Anglo lawyer she works for. "A stellar new play. Searingly funny." –*The New Yorker.* "Both generous and merciless, equally enjoyable and disturbing." –*NY Newsday.* "A bitingly funny new comedy. The plight of working mothers is explored from two pointedly contrasting perspectives in this sympathetic, sensitive new play." –*Variety.* [2M, 6W] ISBN: 0-8222-1994-8

DRAMATISTS PLAY SERVICE, INC.
440 Park Avenue South, New York, NY 10016 212-683-8960 Fax 212-213-1539
postmaster@dramatists.com   www.dramatists.com